P9-AFD-394

Love

A Book of Quotations

Edited by

HERB GALEWITZ

DOVER PUBLICATIONS, INC.
Mineola, New York

DOVER THRIFT EDITIONS

GENERAL EDITOR: PAUL NEGRI

Bibliographical Note

Love: A Book of Quotations is a new work, first published by Dover Publications, Inc., in 1998.

International Standard Book Number: 0-486-40004-2

Manufactured in the United States of America
Dover Publications, Inc., 31 East 2nd Street, Mineola, N.Y. 11501

Note

Everyone has something to say about love, but very little of it is memorable. This book presents just a little of what has been said, but all of it worth remembering. The quotations are from prose, poetry, plays, songs, even conversation. The sources range from ancient times to the 20th century, and from such diverse sensibilities as Dante and Dorothy Parker. The joy and sorrow, pleasure and pain, wisdom and folly, genius and silliness of love all find concise expression in the following pages. The quotations are arranged alphabetically by author.

❧ JOSEPH ADDISON

Mysterious love, uncertain treasure,
Hast thou more of pain or pleasure!
Endless torments, dwell about thee:
Yet who would live, and live without thee.

❧ HENRI FRÉDÉRIC AMIEL

Doubting the reality of love leads to doubting
everything.

True love is that which ennobles the personality,
fortifies the heart, and sanctifies the existence.

❧ SHERWOOD ANDERSON

I am a lover and have not found my thing to
love.

There's a kind of girl you see just once in your
life, and if you don't get busy and make hay then
you're gone for good and all and might as well go
jump off a bridge.

◆§ ANONYMOUS

A poor beauty finds more lovers than husbands.

All's fair in love and war.

Better an old man's darling than a young man's slave.

Follow love and it will flee, flee love and it will follow thee.

Give me a thousand kisses and yet more;
And then repeat those that have gone before.

Happy's the wooing that is not long in doing.

He that would the daughter win,
Must with the mother first begin.

It is a cold sheet that only one person sleeps under.

It will do no man any good to love a woman unless he keeps on telling her so.

Love and smoke cannot be concealed.

Love even teaches asses to dance.

Love in the heart is better than honey in the mouth.

Love is a forger of suspicions.

Love is a passion which comes often we know not how, and which goes also in like manner.

Love is the child of illusion, and the parent of disillusion.

Love laughs at locksmiths.

Love unreciprocated is like a question without an answer.

Maids want nothing but husbands, but when they have them want everything.

Marry in haste, repent in leisure.

Marry the daughter on knowing the mother.

"May I print a kiss on your lips?" I asked;
She nodded her sweet permission;
So we went to press, and I rather guess
We printed a large edition.

May we kiss whom we please
And please whom we kiss.

Nobody loves the way he ought to; he loves the way he has to or is allowed to.

One returns always to his first love.

Perfect love cannot be without equality.

There is more pleasure in loving than in being beloved.

True love suffers no concealment.

When poverty comes in at the door, love flies out the window.

Where the love is great, the pain is great.

Who loves believes the impossible.

Woman: The fairest work of the Great Author; the edition is large, and no man should be without a copy.

✍ JANE AUSTEN

In nine cases out of ten, a woman had better show more affection than she feels.

It is always incomprehensible to a man that a woman should ever refuse an offer of marriage.

It is happy for you that you possess the talent of flattering with delicacy. May I ask whether these pleasing attentions proceed from the impulse of the moment, or are the result of previous study?

⊷§ HONORÉ BALZAC

First love is a kind of vaccination which saves a man from catching the complaint a second time.

It is as absurd to say that a man can't love one woman all the time as it is to say that a violinist needs several violins to play the same piece of music.

Love is to the moral nature exactly what the sun is to the earth.

When women love us, they forgive everything, even our crimes; when they do not love us, they do not credit even our virtues.

Both men & women!

⊷§ JAMES MATTHEW BARRIE

Love is not blind; it is an extra eye, which shows us what is most worthy of regard.

To doubt is to dip love in the mire.

We seldom give our love to what is worthiest in its object.

⊷§ HENRY WARD BEECHER

Young love is a flame; very pretty, often very hot and fierce, but still only light and flickering. The love of the older and disciplined heart is as coals, deep-burning, unquenchable.

✑ ARNOLD BENNETT

Make love to every woman you meet; if you get five per cent on your outlay it's a good investment.

✑ PIERRE JEAN DE BÉRANGER

To love is to be useful to yourself; to cause love is to be useful to others.

✑ AMBROSE BIERCE

Here's to woman! —ah, that we could fall into her arms without falling into her hands!

Kiss, n. A word invented by the poets as a rhyme for "bliss."

✑ JOSH BILLINGS

Friendship is like earthenware, once broken, it can be mended; love is like a mirror, once broken that ends it.

Love is like measles; you can get it only once, and the later in life it occurs the tougher it gets.

Love is said to be blind, but I know lots of fellows in love who can see twice as much in their sweethearts as I can.

❧ WILLIAM BLAKE

Never seek to tell thy love,
Love that never told can be,
For the gentle wind doth move
Silently, invisibly.

❧ BERNARD DE BONNARD

If men knew all that women think, they would
be at least twenty times more audacious.

❧ BOUFLERS

To reason about love is to lose reason.

❧ CHRISTIAN NESTELL BOVEE

Love's sweetest meanings are unspoken; the full
heart know no rhetoric of words, and resorts to
the pantomime of sighs and glances.

Successful love takes a load off our hearts and
puts it on our shoulders.

❧ CHARLOTTE BOWLES

It is not love that steals the heart from love; it is
the hard world and the perplexing cares, its
petrifying selfishness, its pride, its low ambition,
and its paltry aims.

❧ M. E. BRADDON

Why is it so difficult to love wisely, so easy to love too well?

❧ HARRY BRAISTED & STANLEY CARTER

If you want to win her hand,
let the maiden understand
That she's not the only pebble on
the beach!

❧ ANTOINE BRET

The first sigh of love is the last of wisdom.

❧ ROBERT BRIDGES

So sweet love seemed that April morn,
When first we kissed beside the thorn,
So strangely sweet, it was not strange
We thought that love could never change.

❧ HEYWOOD BROUN

The ability to make love frivolously is the chief characteristic which distinguishes human beings from the beast.

❧ ELIZABETH BARRETT BROWNING

How do I love thee? Let me count the ways.

✺§ GEORGE BUCKINGHAM

All true love is grounded on esteem.

✺§ EDWARD GEORGE BULWER-LYTTON

It is astonishing how little one feels poverty when one loves.

It seems to me that the coming of love is like the coming of spring—the date is not to be reckoned by the calendar.

✺§ ROBERT BURNS

But to see her was to love her,
Love but her, and love forever.

It warms me, it charms me,
To mention her name:
It heats me, it beats me,
And sets me a'on flame!

Oh, my luve's like a red, red rose,
That's newly sprung in June.

✺§ ROBERT BURTON

Most part of a lover's life is full of agony, anxiety, fear and grief, complaints, sighs, suspicions, and cares (heigh-ho my heart is full of woe), full of silence and irksome solitariness.

✑ ROGER DE BUSSY-RABUTIN

Absence is to love what wind is to fire; it
quenches the small flame and quickens the large.

Love is a true renewer.

✑ LORD BYRON (GEORGE GORDON)

Alas! the love of women! It is known
To be a lovely and a fearful thing.
I've seen your stormy seas and stormy women,
And pity lovers rather more than seamen.

Love will find its way
Through paths where wolves
Would fear to prey.

Man's love is of man's life a thing apart;
'Tis woman's whole existence.

'Tis melancholy, and a fearful sign
Of human frailty, folly, also crime,
That love and marriage rarely can combine.

Why did she love him? Curious fool —
be still —
Is human love the growth of human
will?

✑ THOMAS CAMPION

Though love and all his pleasures are but toys,
They shorten tedious nights.

↭ THOMAS CARLYLE

If you are ever in doubt as to whether or not you should kiss a pretty girl, always give her the benefit of the doubt.

The first love, which is infinite, can be followed by no second like it.

↭ ALICE CARY

Kiss me, though you make believe;
Kiss me, though I almost know
You are kissing to deceive.

↭ JOYCE CARY

Love doesn't grow on trees like apples in Eden—it's something you have to make. And you must use your imagination to make it too, just like anything else. It's all work, work.

↭ WILLA CATHER

So blind is life, so long at last is sleep,
And none but Love to bid us laugh or weep.

Where are the loves that we have loved before
When once we are alone, and shut the door?

↭ CATULLUS

Let us live, my Lesbia, and love, and value at a penny all the talk of crabbed old men.

What a woman says to her lover should be written on air or swift water.

❧ NICOLAS CHAMFORT

There are two things I have always loved madly: they are women and celibacy.

❧ SEBASTIEN CHAMFORT

The loves of some people are but the result of good suppers.

❧ CHAMISSO

Love embraces woman's whole life; it is her prison and her kingdom of heaven.

❧ LORD CHESTERFIELD

Women who are either indisputably beautiful, or indisputably ugly, are best flattered upon the score of their understandings.

❧ COLLEY CIBER

We shall find no fiend in hell can match the fury of a disappointed woman — scorned, slighted, dismissed without a parting pang.

✍ CALEB CHARLES COLTON

For the love of a woman is a shoot, not a seed, and flourishes most vigorously only when ingrafted on that love which is rooted in the breast of another.

If you cannot inspire a woman with love of you, fill her above the brim with love of herself; all that runs over will be yours.

Most men know what they hate, few what they love.

✍ WILLIAM CONGREVE

A fellow who lives in a windmill has not a more whimsical dwelling than the heart of a man that is lodged in a woman.

Heaven has no rage like love to hatred turned, Nor Hell a fury like a woman scorned.

If there's delight in love, 't is when I see That heart which others bleed for, bleed for me.

✍ PIERRE CORNEILLE

Love rules the earth, subjects the heavens; kings are at his feet; he controls the gods.

When love is satisfied all the charm of it is gone.

✒ Abraham Cowley

But of all pains, the greatest pain
It is to love, but love in vain.

✒ William Cowper

With all thy faults, I love thee still.

✒ F. Marion Crawford

Jealousy is the forerunner of love, and sometimes its awakener.

✒ John Crowne

Poor love is lost in men's capacious minds;
In women's it fill, all the room it finds.

✒ Samual Daniel

Love is a sickness full of woes,
All remedies refusing.

✒ Dante

Love spares no loved one from loving.

✒ Thomas Decker

Love's voice doth sing as sweetly in a beggar as
a king.

❧ DON DICKERMAN

Love: A season's pass on the shuttle between heaven and hell.

❧ BENJAMIN DISRAELI

The magic of first love is the ignorance that it can ever end.

We are all born for love. It is the principle of existence and its only end.

❧ AUSTIN DOBSON

Love comes unseen; we only see it go.

❧ PHILIP DODDRIDGE

If nobody loves you, be sure it is your own fault.

❧ ROBERT DODSLEY

One kind kiss before we part,
Drop a tear and bid adieu;
Though we sever, my fond heart
Till we meet shall pant for you.

❧ MICHAEL DRAYTON

It is your virtue, being men, to try;
And it is ours, by virtue to deny.

✑§ JOHN DRYDEN

Her eyes, her lips, her cheeks, her shape, her features, seem to be drawn by love's own hand, by love himself in love.

Love is love's reward.

Love reckons hours for months, and days for years; and every little absence is an age.

No joys are above
The Pleasures of love.

Pains of love be sweeter far,
Than all other pleasures are.

✑§ MME. DUDEVANT (GEORGE SAND)

Love is the virtue of women.

✑§ RALPH WALDO EMERSON

A believing love will relieve us of a vast load of care.

Here's to the happy man—all the world loves a lover.

Love, and you shall be loved. All love is mathematically just, as much as the two sides of an algebraic equation.

Never self-possessed, or prudent, love is all abandonment.

. . . the sharpest-sighted hunter in the universe is Love for finding what he seeks, and only that.

What is specially true of love is, that it is a state of extreme impressionability; the lover has more senses and finer senses than others.

When the soul flows through a man's affection, it is love.

∾ GERARD DIDIER ERASMUS

Solid love, whose root is virtue, can no more die than virtue itself.

∾ HENRI ÉTIENNE

We always come back to our first loves.

∾ WILLIAM FAULKNER

Perhaps they were right in putting love into books . . . Perhaps it could not live anywhere else.

∾ MADAME FÉE

However dull a woman may be, she will understand all there is in love; however intelligent a man may be, he will never know the half of it.

❧ EDWARD FITZGERALD

A book of Verses underneath the Bough,
A jug of Wine, a Loaf of Bread,—and thou.
Beside me singing in the Wilderness—
Oh! Wilderness were Paradise enow!

❧ ANATOLE FRANCE

In love, a woman lends herself rather than gives herself.

❧ BENJAMIN FRANKLIN

Keep your eyes wide open before marriage; half shut afterwards.

❧ FRENCH PROVERBS

But one always returns to his first love.

Delicacy is to love what grace is to beauty.

It's love that makes the world go 'round.

Love makes time pass. Time makes love pass.

❧ MARGARET WITTER FULLER

It was thy kiss, Love, that made me immortal.
One hour of love will teach a woman more of her true relations than all of your philosophizing.

ৼ JOHN GALSWORTHY

Love is no hot-house flower, but a wild plant, born of a wet night, born of an hour of sunshine; sprung from wild seed, blown along the road by a wild wind.

ৼ RICHARD GARNETT

When Silence speaks for Love she has much to say.

ৼ JOHN GAY

In love we are all fools alike.

If the heart of a man is depress'd with cares, The mist is dispell'd when a woman appears.

ৼ WILLIAM GILBERT

Faint heart never won fair lady.

ৼ JOHANN WOLFGANG VON GOETHE

Any trifle is enough to entertain two lovers.

If I love you, what business is that of yours?

In love all is risk.

Love concedes in a moment what we can hardly attain by effort after years of toil.

Lovers cannot exist without torturing themselves.

That is the true season of love, when we believe that we alone can love, that no one could ever have loved so before us and that no one will love in the same way after us.

Those only obtain love, for the most part, who seek it not.

We are shaped and fashioned by what we love.

What a happiness to be loved! and to love, ye gods, what bliss!

When children, we are sensualists; when in love idealists.

≈§ OLIVER GOLDSMITH

Love is an exotic of the most delicate constitution.

Love must be taken by strategem, not by open force.

Love, when founded in the heart, will show itself in a thousand unpremeditated sallies of fondness.

Suppressing love is but opposing the natural dictates of the heart.

When lovely woman stoops to folly
And finds, too late, that men betray,
What charm can soothe her melancholy?
What art can wash her guilt away?

⊷ GREEK PROVERB

Who love too much, hate in the same extreme.

⊷ JUDGE THOMAS CHANDLER HALIBURTON

The female heart is just like a new india-rubber shoe: you may pull and pull at it till it stretches out a yard long; and then let it go, and it will fly right back to its old shape.

⊷ FITZ-GREENE HALLECK

None knew thee but to love thee,
None named thee but to praise.

⊷ THOMAS HARDY

A lover without indiscretion is no lover at all.

⊷ SYDNEY HARRIS

The only way to understand a woman is to love her — and then it isn't necessary to understand her.

✑ FRANCES R. HAVERGAL

Love understands love: it needs no talk.

✑ WILLIAM HAZLITT

In love we never think of moral qualities, and scarcely of intellectual ones. Temperament and manner alone, with beauty excite love.

✑ HEGGE

Love's like a landscape which doth stand
Smooth at a distance, rough at hand;
Or like a fire which from afar
Doth gently warm, consumes when near.

✑ HEINRICH HEINE

I had a dream long since of Love's wild glow—
Locks, mignonette and myrtle—all it teaches
Of sweet, red kisses and of bitter speeches;
Sad airs of sadder songs—long, long ago!

Silence is the chaste blossom of love.

✑ OLIVER HERFORD

Here's to the Chaperon!
May she learn from Cupid
Just enough blindness
To be sweetly stupid.

❧ ROBERT HERRICK

Love's of itself too sweet; the best of all
Is when love's honey has a dash of gall.

❧ THOMAS KIBBLE HERVEY

A love that took an early root,
And had an early doom.

❧ AARON HILL

She most attracts who longest can refuse.

❧ JOSIAH GILBERT HOLLAND

A woman in love is a very poor judge of
character.

❧ THOMAS HOOD

I love thee, I love thee,
'Tis all that I can say
It is my vision in the night,
My dreaming in the day.

❧ LAURENCE HOUSMAN

Ah! a man's love is strong
When fain he comes a-mating.
But a woman's love is long
And grows when it is waiting.

✍ ELBERT HUBBARD

The love we give away is the only love we keep.

✍ KIN HUBBARD

A chap ought to save a few of the long evenings he spends with his girl till after they're married.

I don't know of anything better than a woman if you want to spend money where it'll show.

✍ VICTOR HUGO

The first symptom of true love in a young man is timidity, in a girl it is boldness. The two sexes have a tendency to approach, and each assumes the qualities of the other.

The supreme happiness of life is the conviction of being loved for yourself, or, more correctly, being loved in spite of yourself.

✍ LEIGH HUNT

Jenny kissed me when we met.
Jumping from the chair she sat in;
Time, you thief! who loves to get
Sweets into your lists, put that in!
Say I'm weary; say I'm sad;
Say that health and wealth missed me;
Say I'm growing old—but add
Jennie kissed me.

⋖§ IRISH PROVERB

Absence makes the heart grow fonder.

⋖§ WASHINGTON IRVING

The love of a delicate female is always shy and silent.

⋖§ ITALIAN PROVERB

Love is an excuse for its own faults.

⋖§ JEROME K. JEROME

Love is like the measles; we all have to go through it.

⋖§ DOUGLAS JERROLD

The surest way to hit a woman's heart is to take aim kneeling.

⋖§ GEORGE JESSEL

Sometimes lack of virility is often mistaken for being hard to get.

⋖§ BASIL JESSHOPE

Senior romance is the second wind you hear,
Its softened whisper lessens fear.

⪥ SAMUEL JOHNSON

 A second marriage is the triumph of hope over experience.

It is commonly a weak man who marries for love.

Love is the wisdom of the fool and the folly of the wise.

Marriage has many pains, but celibacy has no pleasures.

There never was a man who was not gratified by being told that he was liked by the women.

Those that have loved longest love best.

When a man says he had pleasure with a woman he does not mean conversation.

⪥ BEN JONSON

Drink to me only with thine eyes,
And I will pledge with mine;
Or leave a kiss within the cup,
And I'll not look for wine.

⪥ J. A. KARR

Love is the most terrible, and also the most generous of the passions; it is the only one that includes in its dreams the happiness of someone else.

One expresses well only the love he does not feel.

⊷ JOHN KEATS

The day is gone, and its sweets are gone!
Sweet voice, sweet lips, soft hand, and softer
    breast.

⊷ C. KENT

Never speak of love with scorn;
Such were direst treason;
Love was made for eve and morn,
And for every season.

⊷ CHARLES KINGSLEY

Jealousy is often the helpmate of sweet love.

⊷ RUDYARD KIPLING

Cross that rules the Southern sky!
Stars that sweep, and turn, and fly,
Hear the Lover's Litany:—
"Love like ours can never die!"

Heaven grant us patience with a man in love!

The first proof a man gives of his interest in a woman is by talking to her about his own sweet self. If the woman listens without yawning, he begins to like her. If she flatters the animal's vanity, he ends by adoring her.

"They are fools who kiss and tell," wisely hath the poet sung.

❧ ALPHONSE DE LAMARTINE

Passion depraves, but also ennobles.

❧ CHARLES LAMB

Man, while he loves, is never quite depraved.

❧ WALTER SAVAGE LANDOR

Love is a secondary passion in those who love most, a primary in those who love least.

❧ RING LARDNER

He gave her a look that you could of poured on a waffle.

❧ FRANÇOIS, DUC DE LA ROCHEFOUCALD

A man of sense may love like a madman, but not as a fool.

A woman often thinks she regrets the lover, when she only regrets the love.

As in friendship, so in love, we are often happier from ignorance than from knowledge.

In their first passions women are in love with their lover; in the rest, with love.

Jealousy is always born with love, but it does not always die with it.

Prudence and love are not made for each other; as the love increases, prudence diminishes.

The pleasure of love is in loving. We are much happier in the passion we feel than in that we inspire.

True love is like ghosts, which everybody talks about and few have seen.

What makes lovers never tire of each others' society is that they talk always about themselves.

When one loves one doubts even what one most believes in.

⋐§ LATIN PROVERB

All love is vanquished by a succeeding love.

Love begets love.

The falling out of lovers is the renewal of love.

The lover's soul dwells in the body of another.

❧ GEORGETTE LEBLANC

Don't fondle him before meal time—kisses to a hungry man are as soap bubbles to a parched throat.

❧ HENRY SAMBROOKE LEIGH

My love she is a kitten,
and my heart's a ball of string.

❧ GOTTHOLD EPHRAIM LESSING

Equality is the firmest bond of love.

❧ HENRY WADSWORTH LONGFELLOW

Archly the maiden smiled, and, with eyes over-
    running with laughter,
Said, in a tremulous voice, "Why don't you speak
    for yourself, John?"

It is a beautiful trait in the lover's character, that he thinks no evil of the object loved.

It is difficult to know at what moment love begins; it is less difficult to know that it has begun.

Love gives itself; it is not bought.

There is nothing holier in this life of ours than the first consciousness of love, the first fluttering of its silken wings.

When one is truly in love, one not only says it, but shows it.

ⁿ§ ANITA LOOS

"Kissing your hand may make you feel very good but a diamond bracelet lasts forever."

ⁿ§ GEORGE HORACE LORIMER

You spend a year worrying because you think Bill Jones is going to cut you out with your best girl, and then you spend ten worrying because he didn't.

ⁿ§ SAMUEL LOVER

Reproof on her lip, but a smile in her eye.

ⁿ§ LORD LYTTLETON

None without hope e'er lov'd the brightest fair, But love can hope where reason would despair.

୶ GEORGE MacDONALD

Love is the part, and love is the whole;
Love is the robe, and love is the pall;
Ruler of heart and brain and soul,
Love is the lord and the slave of all!

Alas! how easily things go wrong!
A sigh too deep or a kiss too long.
And then comes a mist and a weeping rain,
And life is never the same again.

୶ SYLVAIN MARÉCHAL

Love is like a charming romance which is read
with avidity, and often with such impatience that
many pages are skipped to reach the *dénouement*
sooner.

୶ CHRISTOPHER MARLOWE

Was this the face that launched a thousand
    ships,
And burnt the topless towers of Ilium?
Sweet Helen, make me immortal with a kiss!
Her lips suck forth my soul: see, where it flies!

୶ TOM MASSON

The love game is never called off on account of
darkness.

❧ CHARLES ROBERT MATURIN

'Tis well to be off with the old love
Before you are on with the new.

❧ WILLIAM SOMERSET MAUGHAM

The tragedy of love is indifference.

❧ MELEAGER

O Love that flew so lightly to my heart,
Why are thy wings so feeble to depart?

❧ H. L. MENCKEN

Love is the delusion that one woman differs
from another.

To be in love is merely to be in a state of percep-
tual anaesthesia—to mistake an ordinary young
man for a Greek god or an ordinary young
woman for a goddess.

To the average man, doomed to some banal and
sordid drudgery all his life long, women offer the
only grand hazard that he ever encounters. Take
them away and his existence would be as flat and
secure as that of a milch cow.

ᔥ GEORGE MEREDITH

She whom I love is hard to catch and conquer,
Hard, but O the glory of the winning were she
　　won.

ᔥ JOHN MILTON

Imparadis'd in one another's arms.

Mutual love, the crown of all our bliss.

ᔥ JEAN BAPTISTE POQUELIN MOLIÈRE

We are easily duped by those we love.

ᔥ LADY MARY WORTLEY MONTAGU

Be plain in dress, and sober in your diet;
In short, my deary, kiss me, and be quiet.

ᔥ THOMAS MOORE

If I speak to thee in friendship's name;
Thou think'st I speak too coldly;
If I mention love's devoted flame,
Thou say'st I speak too boldly.

Love must shun the path where many rove;
one bosom to recline upon, one heart to
be his only one, are quite enough for love!

There is nothing half so sweet in life as love's
young dream.

Woman! be fair,—we must adore thee!
Smile,—and a world is weak before thee!

✑§ HANNAH MORE

Absence in love is like water upon fire; a little
quickens, but much extinguishes it.

Love never reasons, but profusely gives—gives,
like a thoughtless prodigal, its all, and trembles
then lest it has done too little.

✑§ E. F. J. MÜNCH-BELLINGHAUSEN

Two souls with but a single thought,
Two hearts that beat as one.

✑§ ALFRED DE MUSSET

Love is a sleep; love is a dream;
you have lived if you have loved.

Partake of love as a temperate man partakes of
wine; do not become intoxicated.

✑§ NAPOLEON

Love is the occupation of the idle man, the
amusement of a busy one, and the shipwreck of a
sovereign.

The only victory over love is flight.

≈ﬞ ALFRED NOYES

I'll come to thee by moonlight, though hell
should bar the way.

≈ﬞ MAX O'RELL

If you want to be on good terms with women,
knock at the door of their vanity, and you will
always find them at home.

In matrimony, love is only *hors d'oeuvre;*
friendship is the *piece de resistance.*

≈ﬞ THOMAS OTWAY

Let us embrace, and from this very moment vow
an eternal misery together.

O woman, lovely woman, nature made thee
To temper man; we had been brutes without you,
Angels are painted fair to look like you.

≈ﬞ OUIDA

Here's to the girl that I love,
And here's to the girl who loves me;
And here's to all that love her whom I love,
And all those who love her who loves me!

❧ OVID

Dignity and love do not blend well, nor do they continue long together.

If any man wish to be idle, let him fall in love.

If thou wishest to put an end to love, attend to business (love yields to employment); then thou wilt be safe.

Love is a credulous affection.

Lovers remember everything.

She half consents who silently denies.

That you may be beloved, be amiable.

There are as many pangs in love as shells on the sea-shore.

❧ DOROTHY PARKER

Men seldom make passes
At girls who wear glasses.

❧ THOMAS PARNELL

Let those love now who never loved before;
Let those who always loved, now love the more.

❦ BLAISE PASCAL

Love has no age, as it is always renewing.

Love is a debt which inclination always pays, obligation never.

❦ JEAN PAUL

Love requires not so much proofs as expressions of love.

Pure love cannot merely do all, but is all.

Time, which deadens hatred, secretly strengthens love.

To love early and marry late is to hear a lark singing at dawn, and at night to eat it roasted for supper.

❦ GEORGE PEELE

They that do change old love for new,
Pray gods, they change for worse.

❦ THOMAS PERCY

Love will find out the way.

Sigh no more, ladies, sigh no more!
Men were deceivers ever;
One foot in sea and one on shore,
To one thing constant never.

✑ PETRARCH

Love accomplishes all things.

✑ PLUTARCH

When the candles are out all women are fair.

✑ EDGAR ALLAN POE

This maiden she lived with no other thought
Than to love and be loved by me.

Years of love have been forgot
In the hatred of a minute.

✑ EDOARDO PONTI

A person who is in love and writes a letter must
remain in love at least until the letter arrives.

✑ ALEXANDER POPE

Fair tresses man's imperial race insnare,
And beauty draws us with a single hair.

For love deceives the best of womankind.

If to her share some female errors fall,
Look on her face, and you'll forget them all.

Love finds an altar for forbidden fires.

Love seldom haunts the breast where learning lies.

Virtue she finds too painful an endeavour,
Content to dwell in decencies forever.

❧ GEORGE DENISON PRENTICE

When a young man complains that a young lady has no heart, it is pretty certain that she has his.

❧ PRINCE DE LIGNE

In love it is only the commencement that charms. I am not surprised that we find pleasure in frequently recommencing.

❧ BRYAN PROCTER

In the darkest spot on earth,
Some love is found.

❧ FRANCIS QUARLES

Convey love to thy friend as an arrow to the mark; not as a ball against the wall, to rebound back again.

❧ WALTER RALEIGH

If all the world and love were young,
And truth in every shepherd's tongue,

Those pretty pleasures might me move
To live with thee, and be thy love.

❧ SAMSON RAPHAELSON

It's impossible to break the heart of a young,
beautiful and healthy woman.

There is no way of getting out of a love affair
that ever succeeds like not getting in.

❧ SAMUEL RICHARDSON

Platonic love is platonic nonsense.

❧ JEAN PAUL RICHTER

Love lessens woman's delicacy and increases
man's.

Love require not so much proofs, as expressions,
of love. Love demands little else than the power
to feel and to requite love.

Paradise is always where love dwells.

❧ EDWARD ARLINGTON ROBINSON

Love must have wings to fly away from love,
And to fly back again.

Love that's wise
Will not say all it means.

❧ MONROE H. ROSENFELD

With all her faults I love her still.

❧ S. ROSSINI

Short is the rapture of love, but eternal is the pain.

❧ JEAN JACQUES ROUSSEAU

To write a good love-letter, you ought to begin without knowing what you mean to say, and to finish without knowing what you have written.

❧ NICHOLAS ROWE

Is she not more than painting can express,
Or youthful poets fancy when they love?

❧ HELEN ROWLAND

In love, somehow, a man's heart is always either exceeding the speed limit, or getting parked in the wrong place.

It is easier to keep half a dozen lovers guessing than to keep one lover after he has stopped guessing.

Marriage: a souvenir of love.

When a girl marries she exchanges the attentions of many men for the inattention of one.

❧ JOHN RUSKIN

From the beginning and to the end of time, Love reads without letters and counts without arithmetic.

❧ HENRY ST. JOHN

Perfect love casteth out fear.

❧ FRIEDRICH VON SCHILLER

He alone knows what love is who loves without hope.

I have enjoyed the happiness of the world; I have lived and loved.

Love is the price of love.

Oh, that it remained for ever green, the fair season of early love.

There is room in the smallest cottage for a happy loving pair.

❧ WALTER SCOTT

Oh, why should man's success remove the very charms that awake his love!

❧ OWEN SEAMAN

No sensible man ever believes that a woman means what she says; and that makes it so much safer to tell the truth.

❧ ERICH SEGAL

Love means not ever having to say you're sorry.

❧ J. P. SENN

Love with old men is as the sun upon the snow, it dazzles more than it warms them.

❧ WILLIAM SHAKESPEARE

All lovers swear more performance than they are able.

As soon go kindle fire with snow, as seek to quench the fire of love with words.

But love is blind, and lovers cannot see
The pretty follies that themselves commit.

Doubt thou the stars are fire;
Doubt that the sun doth move;
Doubt truth to be a liar;
But never doubt I love.

Good night, good night! parting is such sweet
    sorrow,
That I shall say good night 'til it be morrow.

Have you not heard it said full oft,
A woman's nay doth stand for naught?

If music be the food of love, play on.

If thou wilt needs marry, marry a fool.

Is it not strange that desire should so many years
outlive performance?

Jealousy: It is the green-eyed monster that doth
    mock
The meat it feeds on.

Kindness in women, not their beauteous looks,
Shall win my love.

Let me not to the marriage of true minds
Admit impediments. Love is not love
Which alters when it alteration finds.

Love is a smoke made with fume of sighs.

Love looks not with the eyes, but with the mind.

Love moderately; long love doth so;
Too swift arrives as tardy as too slow.

Love sought is good, but given unsought is
better.

Men are April when they woo,
December when they wed.

My bounty is as boundless as the sea, my love
as deep; the more I give to thee, the more I have,
for both are infinite.

O, that I were a glove upon that hand,
That I might touch that cheek!

Prosperity is the very bond of love.

She is a woman, therefore may be woo'd;
She is a woman, therefore may be won.

She is mine own;
And I as rich in having such a jewel
As twenty seas, if all their sand were pearl.

Speak low, if you speak love.

Stony limits cannot hold love out.

Sweet, good night!
This bud of love, by summer's ripening breath,
May prove a beauteous flower when next we
   meet.

The course of true love never did run smooth.

The kiss you take is better than you give.

Then must you speak
Of one who loved not wisely but too well.

There lives in the very flame of love
A kind of wick or snuff that doth abate it.

There's beggary in the love that can be
reckoned.

They do not love, that do not show their love.

They love least, that let men know their love.

When love speaks, the voice of all the gods,
Makes heaven drowsy with the harmony.

Win her with gifts if she respect not words;
Dumb jewels, often in their silent kind,
More quick than words, do move a woman's
    mind.

Wish chastely, and love dearly.

You are my true and honorable wife;
As dear to me as the ruddy drops
That visit my heart.

⇜ GEORGE BERNARD SHAW

The fickleness of women I love is only equaled
by the infernal constancy of the women who love
me.

The ideal love affair is one conducted by post.

❧ WILLIAM SHENSTONE

Love-verses, writ without any real passion, are the most nauseous of all conceits.

❧ RICHARD BRINSLEY SHERIDAN

Is not music the food of love?

❧ HERBERT SHIPMAN

Across the gateway of my heart
I wrote "No Thoroughfare,"
But love came laughing by, and cried:
"I enter everywhere."

❧ PHILIP SIDNEY

My true love hath my heart, and I have his,
By just exchange one for the other given:
I hold his dear, and mine he cannot miss,
There never was a better bargain driven.

❧ ISAAC BASHEVIS SINGER

Sometimes love is stronger than a man's convictions.

⋐ ARABELLA EUGENIA SMITH

Keep not your kisses for my dead, cold brow;
The way is lonely, let me feel them now.

⋐ LOGAN PEARSALL SMITH

Unrequite affections seem in youth unmitigated
woes; only later do we learn to appreciate the
safe, sad charms of these bogus heartbreaks.

⋐ SYDNEY SMITH

To love and be loved is the greatest happiness of
existence.

⋐ WALTER SMITH

Love waits for love, though the sun be set,
And the Stars come out, the dews are wet,
And the night-winds moan.

⋐ SOCRATES

The hottest love has the coldest end.

⋐ BISHOP ROBERT SOUTH

Love covers a multitude of sins.

∽ THOMAS SOUTHERNE

For love is but discovery,
When that is made, the pleasure is done.

∽ ROBERT SOUTHEY

What will not woman, gentle woman, dare,
When strong affection stirs her spirit up!

∽ EDMUND SPENSER

All for love; and nothing for reward.

∽ MADAME DE STAEL

Love which is only an episode in the life of man,
is the entire history of woman's life.

Nothing in love can be premeditated; it is as a
power devine, that thinks and feels within us,
unswathed by our control.

∽ RICHARD STEELE

Though her mien carries much more invitation
than command, to behold her is an immediate
check to loose behavior; to love her was a liberal
education.

∽ ABEL STEPHENS

Only those who love with the heart can animate
the love of others.

❧ LAURENCE STERN

Courtship consists in a number of quiet attentions, not so pointed as to alarm, nor so vague as
not to be understood.

❧ ROSE PASTOR STOKES

Some pray to marry the man they love,
My prayer will somewhat vary:
I humbly pray to heaven above
That I love the man I marry.

❧ JOHN SUCKLING

Out upon it, I have loved
Three whole days together;
And am like to love three more,
If it prove fair weather.

Why so pale and wan, fond lover?
Prithee, why so pale?
Will, when looking well can't move her,
Looking ill prevail?

❧ JONATHAN SWIFT

As love without esteem is capricious and
volatile, esteem without love is languid and cold.

In men desire begets love, and in women love
begets desire.

Lord, I wonder what fool it was that first
invented kissing.

Love is a bottomless pit; it is a cormorant —
a harpy that devours everything.

ᛒ ALGERNON CHARLES SWINBURNE

Ah, beautiful passionate body
That never has ached with a heart!

And the best and the worst of this is
That neither is most to blame,
If you've forgotten my kisses,
And I've forgotten your name.

Then love was the pearl of his oyster,
And Venus rose red out of the wine.

ᛒ ARTHUR SYMONS

And I would have, now love is over,
An end to all, an end:
I cannot, having been your lover,
Stoop to become your friend!

ᛒ SYRUS

The anger of lovers renews the strength of love.

✣ CHARLES TALLEYRAND-PÉRIGORD

Love is a reality which is born in the fairy region of romance.

✣ ALFRED LORD TENNYSON

In the spring a young man's fancy lightly turns to thoughts of love.

Let love be free; free love is for the best.

Marriages are made in heaven.

O love! O fire! once he drew
With one long kiss my whole soul through
My lips, as sunlight drinketh dew.

She stood a sight to make an old man young.

Tis better to have loved and lost
Than never to have loved at all.

To love one maiden only, cleave to her,
And worship her by years of noble deeds,
Until they won her.

Who are wise in love, love most, say least.

Who shuts love out shall be shut out from love.

∽§ TERENCE

A man can be so changed by love as to be unrecognizable as the same person.

The quarrels of lovers bring about a renewal of love.

∽§ WILLIAM MAKEPEACE THACKERY

Love makes fools of us all, big and little.

Remember, it is as easy to marry a rich woman as a poor woman.

∽§ FRANCIS THOMPSON

I fear to love you, Sweet, because Love's the ambassador of loss.

∽§ HARRY VON TILZER

Down lover's lane we'll wander,
sweetheart, you and I;
Wait till the sun shines, Nellie,
bye and bye.

I love my wife, but oh you kid.

I want a girl just like the girl that married dear old dad.

❧ LEO TOLSTOY

To say that you can love one person all your life is just like saying that one candle will continue burning as long as you live.

❧ SYDNEY TREMAYNE

A love affair that never ends is one that has been interrupted.

All women want real love, but their passion for bargains leads them to accept cheap imitations.

As soon as a woman has put a man in her power she puts him out of her heart.

Even the most upright man may be tempted by a recumbent woman.

Flirtation is the froth on top of the wine of love.

It is a funny thing that a man always has to tell a woman that he loves her while everyone else knows it without being told.

It is a woman's lot to pretend to care less than she does, while a man pretends to care more than he does. They both leave off pretending about the same time.

Love is a thirst that one cannot quench without becoming intoxicated.

Love is like a bazaar. The admittance is free but it costs something before you get out.

A man does not ask a woman if she loves him until he is almost sure that she does so, and a woman does not ask a man if he loves her until she is almost sure that he does so no longer.

A man will tell a woman that he loves her for herself alone, but what he really means is that he loves her for himself alone.

Most women start a love affair by having a secret with a man, and end by having secrets from him.

There are three stages in a man's infatuation for a woman: making his way, having his way, and going his way.

There are two sorts of men, those who are constant in love and those who are constantly in love—and perhaps the first don't exist.

Women love men for what they give them, men love women for what they deny them.

SAMUEL TUKE

He is a fool who thinks by force or skill
To turn the current of a woman's will.

❧ PAUL VALERY

The real value of love is the increased general vitality it produces.

❧ H. VINCENT

I am not one of those who do not believe in love at first sight, but I believe in taking a second look.

❧ VIRGIL

Cruel love! what is there to which thou dost not drive mortal hearts?

Love conquers all the world, let us too yield to love.

❧ VOLTAIRE

All the reasonings of men are not worth one sentiment of women.

God created woman only to tame men.

Love is a canvas furnished by nature and embroidered by imagination.

Pleasure has its time; so, too, has wisdom. Make love in thy youth, and in old age attend to thy salvation.

ARTEMUS WARD

Alas, she married another. They frequently do. I hope she is happy—because I am.

JOHN GREENLEAF WHITTIER

But love has never known a law
Beyond its own sweet will.

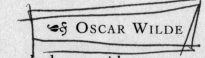

OSCAR WILDE

A man can be happy with any woman as long as he does not love her.

I am sick of women who love me. Women who hate me are much more interesting.

. . . love and gluttony justify everything.

Love is an illusion.

Men always want to be a woman's first love. That is their clumsy vanity. Women have a more subtle instinct about things: What they like is to be a man's last romance.

. . . not love at first sight, but love at the end of the season, which is so much more satisfactory.

One should always be in love. That is the reason one should never marry.

She'll never love you unless you are always at
her heels; women like to be bothered.

The only difference between a caprice and a life-
long passion is that the caprice lasts a little
longer.

To love oneself is the beginning of a life-long
romance.

What a silly thing love is! It is not half as useful
as logic, for it does not prove anything and it is
always telling one things that are not going to
happen, and making one believe things that are
not true.

Women are meant to be loved, not to be understood.

Women love us for our defects. If we have
enough of them, they will forgive us everything,
even our own gigantic intellects.

The London season is entirely matrimonial;
people are either hunting for husbands or hiding
from them.

Twenty years of romance makes a woman look
like a ruin; but twenty years of marriage makes
her something like a public building.

When you really want love you will find it
waiting for you.

☙ THYRA SAMTER WINSLOW

Platonic love is love from the neck up.

☙ P. G. WODEHOUSE

Where one goes wrong when looking for the ideal girl is in making one's selection before walking the full length of the counter.

☙ WILLIAM WORDSWORTH

Love betters what is best.

☙ HENRY WOTTON

Love lodged in a woman's breast
Is but a guest.